TALKS OF HEART

— Aayushi Bhawan

FOR

My parents, without whom I would never have
been able to find words,
My brother, who has always appreciated me
in the most innocent ways,
My one true friend who was actually my first
listener when it came to my writings
&
Last but never the least,
My motivator and My bestest friend without
whom this wouldn't have been possible!

By Aayushi Bhawan

CONTENT

<u>CONTENT</u>

@JUSTASTROKEE
By Aayushi Bhawan

IT'S THE ESSENCE!

It's not the sense that has to make sense
It's the essence!
The one true real meaning
That has to come out from whatever you do
That actually adds up to humankind
That actually teaches people to be kind
The one that never forgets it roots
The one that is bigger than all the fake
truths...
It's the essence!

By Aayushi Bhawan

TWIDDLE

To feel a feeling
Is to have that fire in you
That keeps you so alive
To let go of all the desires in you!

It is to have that contagious depth
That not everybody is gifted with
As their realms aren't shifted with
To not to enclose it with balky
It might make our shoulders bulky
In order to make everything silky
One should stop getting sulky
It is all easy once one takes a deep breathe
Making some tea and taking some rest!

To feel a feeling
Is to have that fire in you
That keeps you so alive
Spirituality wires in you!

SEA SHORE

Serve or curse
Mess or bless
Cure or endure
It's always beneath the sea shore...

By Aayushi Bhawan

SOFT SPOT

Choose Love
When you see no one beside you
When you know that you are at times by yourself
And to feel busy you keep your face inside those
book shelves
Choose Love...

Choose Love
Because every angry, tired, frustrated being wants
it
Because every innocent voice ever heard yearns it
Because every rebel unintentionally did once burn it
Choose Love...

Choose Love
Simply because it's the only original feeling in the
world
Makes you want to feel it again and again and
again
And to give it out to others as much as possible not
with the intention to gain
So Choose Love...

BLOOMING

With all the darkness around me,
I keep the light in me alive,
It gives me a reason to see things a
bit differently,
A reason simply to thrive!

By Aayushi Bhawan

MORALE

A trait not everybody can master
If done a bit over, can become a disaster
But one simply becomes a gangster after
Confidence is what we call it
Which is not laid easily on everybody's
platter!

I PEEKED!

How beautiful it could have been
If my eyes forever stared in his eyes
Without blinking even for once
Because that's what I crave for
The depth, the warmth, the little held
As if the eyes are enough for me to hold him
As if I know what's in his mind
As if I know what's in his heart that I might
find,
As if I know what's itching him
As if I know what's weeping in him
I don't say much but
I want to let him know
I do see him...

By Aayushi Bhawan

SPECIAL TRIBE

Yess I love them more than anybody ever can
I care for them
I caress them
I cherish them
I cry for them

I smile for them
I crave them
I discuss with them
I describe to them

I argue with them
I fight with them
I fight for them
I fly because of them
Yess I love them more than anybody ever can!

SWEET POISON

The intake of it feels good
As I think it should
If one would know the effect of it
I typically crave for it
Knowing the harm it'll cause
Remembering that I take a pause
But put it in my mouth feeling
That this is it that I am capable of deserving
Having it can satisfy others
Who want to see me in pain
I won't show it
It might itch their vein
I take it so that I am reminded
That hurt is all I'll ever gain
The process will take some time
The beautiful crime
Of killing the insides of my chime
Because for others it'll taste like lime
Well to make it purely sugary
Maybe I should call it
'The sweet potion mime'...

By Aayushi Bhawan

PERSONAGE

Worth is worthy when worthiness implies
It hears it's shears but then it denies
Denies to the extent where one won't be able to
rise The who survives this meets with a prize

Worth is worthy when worthiness implies
It cries, it thrives because it truly drives
Drives to the end where one could pay the price
If it doesn't reaches the destination, soon it dies

Worth is worthy when worthiness implies
It defines, it shines as it shows the wise
Wise enough that no ordinary buys
Worthy-Wisey, we can together make it our hymes...

AT ODDS...

The only unlikeness between you and I
Is that you wanted the light
Whereas I cared more upon finding the light,
You wanted to see trees
Where I wanted to first plant saplings,
You wanted to let the details go
Where I wanted to dive in them and then float,
You simply wanted everything already there
Where all I wanted for you is to see me get ready
and stare,
You see, you and I, we come from the different
dimensions of the world,
Where I completely understand what you want
But all I ever really needed was for you to just
hold

The only unlikeness between you and I!

By Aayushi Bhawan

FUTILE

In vain it goes,
The feelings, the efforts, the mindful chores,
Bickering is all I hear
After the emotions worth a crore

In vain it goes,
The steeps, the weeps, in air it blows
More than enough too is never really enough
Learning this I found myself froze

In vain it goes,
The time, the rhyme, as they doze
Unseen, Unheard is when one writes
But no-one cares is what it clearly shows

In vain it goes,
The dots then the thoughts, in the water it
floats If appreciated just enough
It's than just growth and glows...

ARDENCY

Nothing can be compared to the thought that
every soul is complete in itself
And we tend to take it so easily...

By Aayushi Bhawan

TO BE THE LAST...

To be the first I got to know was such
an easy charge
But to be the last my friend,
The last clearly states the only
Never lonely
Because it's homely
So holy
Uncanny
Super silly and jungly
To be lively
Kindly unwindly
Very slowly and steadily and softly
To be, infact, is deathly
Yet lovely
Everlastingly
To be the last...

LITTLE MISS QUIRKY!

Little Miss Quirky
Is often quite
Until she finds the energy,
A spark of light
The one that's pretty bright,
The one that is just alright,
The one worth the fight,
The one she knows deep down is
absolutely right,
Little Miss Quirky
Is till then quite!

By Aayushi Bhawan

UTTER SOLITUDE

After crying is the best sleep you'll ever
get It's peace for next few hours I can bet
It can make you forget all the offsets
It makes your mind ready and set
For another day which you don't want to
regret
Cause you don't want to meet the demon
that you met
It might bring one's life's forever sunset
Although all the sunset lovers, I don't want
to upset
For being the one who loves them too,
I will try to commute the mindset
And yet
After crying is the best sleep you'll ever get!

TOWARDS MISERY

I want to feel anything
But not the pain
Please, not the pain
It tells me everytime I feel minimal joy
That it'll come back
As if it keeps haunting me
As if the only feeling I deserve to feel
Is this
As if anything other than this
Is not meant for me
If it is
Then please come rescue me
I want to feel anything
But not the pain...

By Aayushi Bhawan

TRULY FROM THEIR CORES!

We are not what we suffered
We are from what we conquered
In the process of such suppression and repression
We chose nothing but to accept imperfections
Choosing to love which wasn't loved earlier
He who feels this, feels surreal
How humble of us to make him feel
The joy he actually deserved
When he was left not to be even observed
So be kind to the silent roars
Because they are truly from their cores!

UNLEARN TO LEARN

We live on a globe
Where from our families is what we
learn what to learn
And from the world
We learn what not to learn!

By Aayushi Bhawan

BEAUTY SPOT OF EARTH

Astounded by the moon
I am
The gaze I feel of it when I start spilling
secrets
The silence that it allows me to say
more The way it talks back to me with
the help of clouds
Astounded by the moon
I am!

LOVE? WHAT I SEE?
LOVE? WHAT YOU SEE?

How can I sleep when I know that
He's weeping
I am the reason behind the tears
Is enough to simply kill me
The pain I feel, the pain he feels
Is inevitably harmful
Yet we keep our faces joyful
Pretending all this in front of others
When we both see the wars we fight within
For ourselves, With ourselves
Merely just to ensure and assure and reassure
That we truly will find ourselves
By that sea shore...

By Aayushi Bhawan

WOUNDS BY SNAKES

They say words have no power
I say they hurt more than any dagger
To be able to pierce right into the nerve
Rather now I would say words hurt less,
Actually, it's the attacker!

MISADVENTURE

Only if something disastrous would happen
Is when they'll look upon you?
If something hazardous would cause
Is when they'll hook upon you?
Only if it is visibly visible
Is when they'll reassure you?
Such a shame it is that fantasizing such mishaps
are now the reality
In which only they might be a little good to
you...

By Aayushi Bhawan

TOAST TO THE FORGIVERS!

Shoutout to the forgivers in the world
You make this Earth a better place
Soulfully and emotionally rich
To them, they value their withins the
most,
So stand up for them and raise the
toast!

THE ULTIMATE IGNITE...

Afflicting loudly takes courage
To be brave enough to have that loud ache inside
and yet the voice is strident and coherent
Heard outside
The inner suffer shouldn't dim the inner light
To be precise, actually it should be as if
The Ultimate Ignite...

By Aayushi Bhawan

MAA

Nourishing and Nurturing is the
sweet trap
She'll know what's wrong with a
quick snap
Listen her cause she'll guide you
in life like a go-to map
Now go run and sleep in her lap
ASAP!

TRUE SOUL

How beautiful is the person who simply finds
beauty even in the blackness of the world!
Makes sure that he keeps on looking for it no
matter what the future holds!
The one who has this ability is not fragile but
only bold...
Because his thoughts, his beliefs, his values
are worth that of gold!

By Aayushi Bhawan

BEHOLDEN

This, that I felt
You have no idea how good that night
I slept
It was all joyous tears that I wept
I even imagined how carefully I was
held
In the unreal arms I did then melt
Because nobody noticed how badly I
wanted to be kept
Right there...

ULTRAGE

Only if I could find words to describe this emotion of mine
It's a bit tough I know but I will be fine
Only if feelings and emotions
Were as straight as a line
And only if I could share it all with you over a glass of wine...

It's always been boiling in me
It's always like nerves dismantling and then joining in me
It has never ever been rejoicing me
But has been rapidly destroying me...

It bursts like a lava inside
Burns like a volcano beside
Bears me with all I abide
Bangs like a hammer here in my mind...

All that I could think about is this
And oh my my it's definitely not a bliss
This emotion can always bring reminisce
But all this can cool me down with just one kiss...

By Aayushi Bhawan

WHAT IF?

What if it doesn't go the way we want
and then it haunts?
What if it becomes brutal and we become
cruel?
What if we cut each other with words
and then cry while the other hurts?
What if it becomes 'You' and 'I' and
'We' just can't deny?
What if we want each other but can't
because of one another?
What if?

ITS EITHER USE OR ABUSE!

It's either use or abuse
For men it's definitely juice
Lust is all over their fuse
But they portray as it's love just for the views

It's either use or abuse
Be it standing in a queue
Or hands wander under while we chew
Or maybe in a washroom cause
Nobody will have any kinda clue

It's either use or abuse
For the sake of some blues
Or maybe for some good news
It most of the times leaves an invisible
bruise Cause it's either use or abuse...

By Aayushi Bhawan

TO BE

To be your patience in this impatient world
To be your essence in this nonsense world
To be your eyes in this blind world
To be your ears in this unheard world
To be your go-to stop in this busy world
To be your weekend in this weakly world
To be your wholesome in this vile world
To be your one and only in this heedless world

To be yours and only yours...

SILENCE

Only if you hear,
You know that silence speaks
It keeps you dead and alive
For thousands of weeks

Silence being so weak
It keeps you numb
Doesn't let you grow
Like a sweet little plum

Silence being so powerful
If keeps one up-righteous
Not only it compells
It blows up people's sirens

Only if you hear
You know that silence speaks
It keeps you dead and alive
For thousands of weeks...

By Aayushi Bhawan

MY ALMOST

The word that will tear you apart
The meaning that could mean dispart
The word you'll hate the most
Is called ALMOST...

Means nothing but something you now only shed,
Nothing but something you put under your head
Nothing but you wouldn't want to live without
Nothing but now you have to live without...

Everything that is his little nuisance
Everything that is his impatience
Everything that is his fragrance
Everything that is his silence...

Yes
He's my almost,
My uttermost,
MY ALMOST...

WHY?

Why is it that one has to go through pain
To gain any gain?
Why has the nature turned out to be so cruel
That it had to drain the roots of nurture's
fuel?
Why is the feeling of ignorance still present
Knowing it can cause immense level of
resentment?
WHY?

By Aayushi Bhawan

BURNESS

Burness is what I am now
Burnt nest is all that's left
No matter who may come and go
Burning is all what I had to feel but how?

How do I tell myself that you can't burn?
How do I tell myself that you can't yearn?
When all I ever did was to want and want that feeling
How do I tell myself that you can't take that turn?

The turn that might destroy you
The turn that will deploy you
The turn that I can't take even if I want to
But that turn might sweetly annoy you...

Burness is what I am now
Burnt nest is all that's left
No matter who may come and go
Burning is all that I now allow!

YOU AMUSE ME!

You amuse me
Yes you
With all that you hold within
It's in your bone and skin
I know it's actually violin
And they think it'll be fine with a bottle of gin
Well for a minute or two it could be
A day or two too would be
But actually according to me
It is not the key
To this lock
Will need a pair of ears and eyes
Which will see what is to their surprise
The ones who show you
Their back will never find
The ones who cried with you
Will know you are one of a kind...

By Aayushi Bhawan

MOONFLOWER

To follow the light on the bright path of life is
quite a brilliant venture,
To find a light in the darkest path of life is a
hell of an adventure!

MY MATE!

Speechless is what I am when it comes to you
Never thought this would happen
We stick like glue
You came in my world
And then boom!
Don't want you to ever exit
Cause together we'll bloom!

By Aayushi Bhawan

PEACE

Sleep is my only dopamine
Nothing's more peaceful than this line
Considered it the most
It's the easiest excuse to ghost
Don't let anyone tell you otherwise
It should be declared as the global
prize Now let me take a quick nap
In her blissful lap!

DISCONNECT?

What if the lines we withdraw
Joins us...

By Aayushi Bhawan

GRIEF

Grief I assume is the purest form of love
It shows it actually is all and above
It makes one quiver and shiver for the other
half of ourself
Then you are left with the memories of the
your true self!

HE

He is the poetry I write everyday
Just to erase it again and again and
again...

By Aayushi Bhawan

FIRE

Fire is she
Soothing enough to
Keep you warm
Yet
Fierce enough to
Sway you away like a storm...

ART

A father's soul
A mother's heart
Combined together
Is a work of art!

By Aayushi Bhawan

THE ETERNAL PULL

The eternal pull that you feel
It has the power through which anybody can heal
Look within you'll find yourself
Read the books that are lying on the shelf Dare
not to allow anybody to say
You are not a beam of ray
Believe in what you feel
Cause then you'll become the ideal!

ABSOLUTE NOTHINGNESS...

Into the absolute nothingness
Is actually where we stand
The black-blue sky above
Is where the living holds hand
To find meaning in it
Is what will be called grand
Bring out life from
Is how we'll expand
Selfish uses of natural resources
Should be banned
How come it hasn't teared
Every bone every gland
Respecting females should be a subject
On this motherland
So let's come together
With our human band
And make something so solid
From absolute sand!

By Aayushi Bhawan

A CHANCE BY HIM

Given you is a chance by him
This human body and each skim!

Don't you loose it over a silly thought
Fight those inner battles that
None would have fought
Become a being for yourself to be proud upon
Then keep on doing it
Go on and on and on
Stop only to start again
Quitting was never in your vein
To become someone who you,
Your future kids and their future kids will
look upto
Never take a step back and undo

Given you is a chance by him
This human body and each skim!

INARTICULATE

You want me as much as I do
Cause we know all that we came through
Now is all that we want
You and me folded in our arms
So badly and tight
Nobody could ever separate us
Even if to
Only our bodies would
Our souls would still be hugging each other just right
The longing won't be for much long now
Cause we know the who, when and how
Desparately wanting to breathe our breathes
Just to breathe enough all at once
It's the fuel basically
That keeps us alive and still typically
Not that we can't stay away from each other
But definitely not for too long
This is how much I am missing you
Maybe one day I won't because beside you
Is where I belong
Cause we know all that we came through
You want me as much as I do...

By Aayushi Bhawan

HUSH-HUSH WIN!

Not feeling anything
Yet feeling everything
In my head it rings
In my heart it stings
My heartbeat strums some strings
That's why my voice sings
Because I know in the end,
My soul wins!

POETRY? POET

To the ones who want to be the
poetry and not the poet for once,
I see you and I hear you
But I dare not to understand you
Because to be a poetry is all about
tragedy
But to be a poet my friend,
Now that's something bigger than
any prodigy...